T0378636

15-Minute Foodie

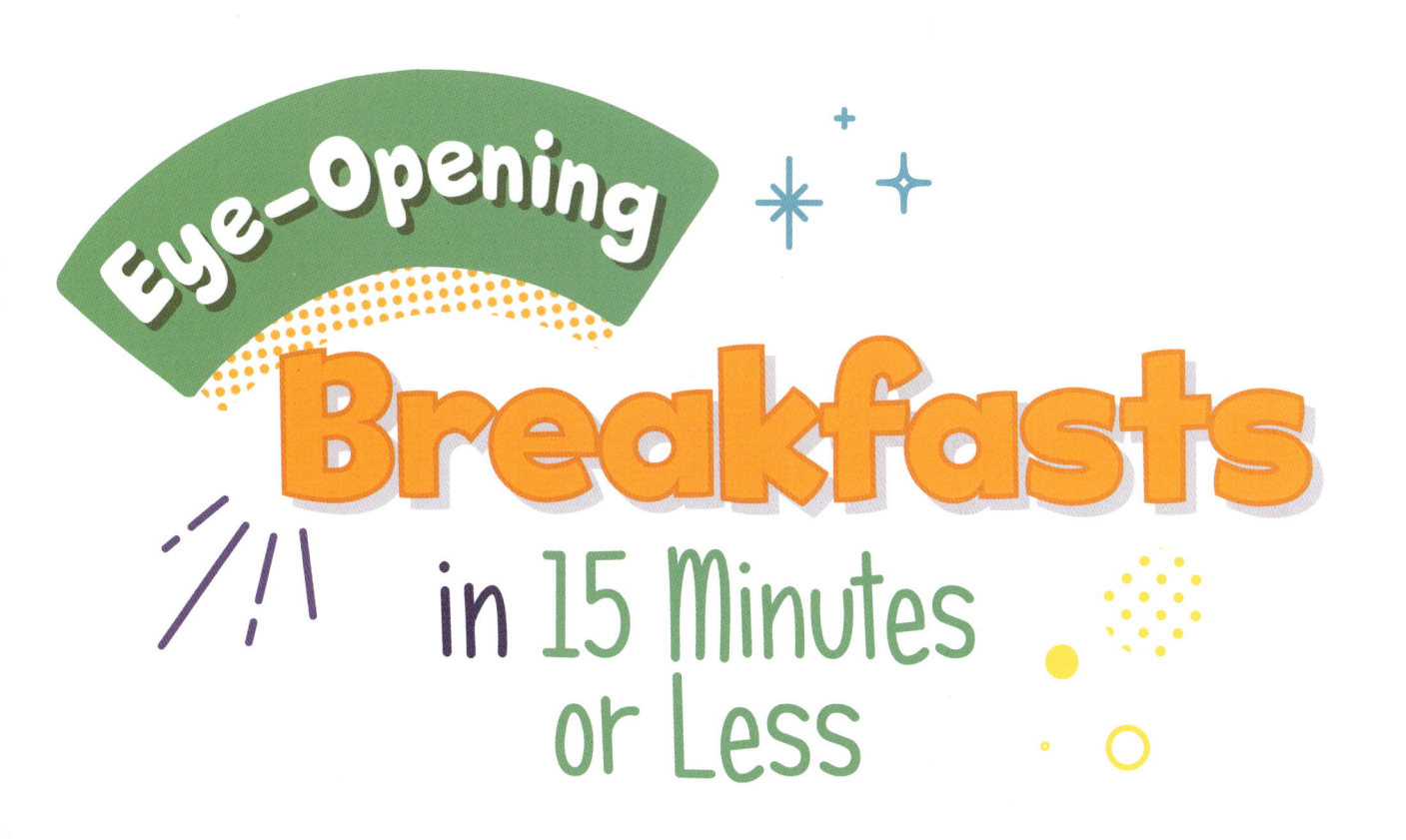

Eye-Opening Breakfasts in 15 Minutes or Less

by Tamara JM Peterson

CAPSTONE PRESS
a capstone imprint

Dabble Lab is published by Capstone Press, an imprint of Capstone.
1710 Roe Crest Drive, North Mankato, Minnesota 56003
capstonepub.com

Library of Congress Cataloging-in-Publication Data
Names: Peterson, Tamara JM, author.
Title: Eye-opening breakfasts in 15 minutes or less / by Tamara JM Peterson.
Description: North Mankato, Minnesota : Capstone Press, a Capstone imprint, [2024] |
Series: 15-minute foodie | Includes bibliographical references. | Audience: Ages 8-11 |
Audience: Grades 4-6 | Summary: "Looking to start your day with a quick and delicious breakfast? Become a 15-minute foodie! Heat up a hearty batch of peanut butter and jelly oatmeal. Make the world's easiest omelet with a mug and a microwave. Serve up a fruity yogurt parfait in a crispy wonton wrapper. These quick, fun, yummy recipes will be ready to savor in 15 minutes or less"— Provided by publisher.
Identifiers: LCCN 2023023927 (print) | LCCN 2023023928 (ebook) |
ISBN 9781669061595 (hardcover) | ISBN 9781669061557 (pdf) |
ISBN 9781669061571 (kindle edition) | ISBN 9781669061564 (epub)
Subjects: LCSH: Breakfasts—Juvenile literature. | Quick and easy cooking—Juvenile literature. | LCGFT: Cookbooks.
Classification: LCC TX733 .P43 2024 (print) | LCC TX733 (ebook) |
DDC 641.5/2—dc23/eng/20230524
LC record available at https://lccn.loc.gov/2023023927
LC ebook record available at https://lccn.loc.gov/2023023928

Image Credits
Adobe Stock: bernardbodo, 5, soleg, 4, xamtiw, Front Cover (granola); Mighty Media, Inc.: 15 (oats), project photos

Design Elements
iStockphoto: Sirintra_Pumsopa, yugoro; Mighty Media, Inc.

Editorial Credits
Editor: Jessica Rusick
Designers: Sarah DeYoung and Denise Hamernik
Cooks: Tamara JM Peterson and Chelsey Luciow

Printed and bound in China. 5593

Table of Contents

Eye-Opening Breakfasts in Fifteen!

Are you looking for eye-opening breakfasts to add some excitement to your mornings? Whether you're in the mood for pancakes, eggs, donuts, or waffles, this book is full of ideas to satisfy your cravings. And the best part is, these recipes come together in 15 minutes or less! So grab your kitchen supplies and read through the tips on the next page. Soon enough, you'll be a 15-minute foodie!

Basic Supplies

baking sheet

blender

frying pan

knife and cutting board

measuring cups and spoons

mixing bowls

muffin tin

spatula

spoon

waffle iron

whisk

Kitchen Tips

Ask an adult for permission before you make a recipe.

Read through the recipe and set out all ingredients and supplies before you start cooking.

Using metric tools? Use the conversion chart below to make your recipe measure up.

Wash your hands before and after you handle food. Wash and dry fresh produce before use.

Ask an adult for help when using a knife, blender, or stovetop. Wear oven mitts when removing items from the oven or microwave.

When you are done making food, clean your work surface. Wash dirty dishes and put all supplies and ingredients back where you found them.

Standard	Metric
¼ teaspoon	1.25 grams or milliliters
½ teaspoon	2.5 g or mL
1 teaspoon	5 g or mL
1 tablespoon	15 g or mL
¼ cup	57 g (dry) or 60 mL (liquid)
⅓ cup	75 g (dry) or 80 mL (liquid)
½ cup	114 g (dry) or 125 mL (liquid)
⅔ cup	150 g (dry) or 160 mL (liquid)
¾ cup	170 g (dry) or 175 mL (liquid)
1 cup	227 g (dry) or 240 mL (liquid)
1 quart	950 mL

Tropical Smoothie

Start the morning like you're on vacation! Blend a simple yet delicious tropical smoothie for a taste of paradise.

Ingredients

½ cup pineapple chunks
½ cup mango chunks
½ cup banana slices
½ cup coconut milk
½ tablespoon coconut
   flakes (optional)

Supplies

knife and cutting board
measuring cups and
   spoons
blender
tall glass

Food Tip

This recipe will
work with frozen,
canned, or fresh
fruit.

1. Put the fruit into the blender.

2. Add the coconut milk to the blender. Blend for three to four minutes or until the mixture is smooth.

3. Pour the smoothie into the glass.

4. If you'd like, garnish the smoothie with coconut flakes and a banana slice. Enjoy!

Apple & Date Bites

Looking for a quick and healthy breakfast? These tasty bites will give you the energy you need to start the day right.

Ingredients

1 cup dried apples
½ cup pitted dates
½ cup almonds
½ cup rolled oats
½ cup hot water, plus
  extra as needed
1 tablespoon maple syrup
1 teaspoon cinnamon

Supplies

measuring cups and
  spoons
blender
spatula (if needed)
spoon
parchment paper
baking sheet

1. Put all the ingredients into the blender.

2. Blend the ingredients on high speed until the mixture has a doughlike consistency. If the mixture becomes too thick to blend, stop the blender and scrape down the sides with the spatula. Then add more water 1 tablespoon at a time, blending between each one, until the mixture thins.

3. Scoop out the mixture 1 tablespoon at a time. Roll the scoops into balls and set them on the parchment-lined baking sheet.

4. Place the apple and date bites into the freezer for 10 minutes. Then dig in!

Breakfast Bruschetta

Bruschetta is a savory Italian appetizer. Put a sweet breakfast spin on bruschetta with honey, cream cheese, and berries!

Ingredients

1 baguette
8 ounces cream cheese
2 tablespoons honey
4 to 5 strawberries, sliced
mint leaves cut into
    ribbons, plus extra for
    garnish

Supplies

knife and cutting board
parchment paper
baking sheet
measuring spoons
bowl
spoon

1. Preheat the oven to 350 degrees Fahrenheit (177 degrees Celsius). Slice the baguette into rounds and place them on the parchment-lined baking sheet. Put the baking sheet in the oven for five minutes to warm.

2. Mix the cream cheese and honey in the bowl.

3. Remove the baguette rounds from the oven.

4. Spread the honey cream cheese on the baguette rounds.

5. Top the rounds with the strawberries.

6. Add the mint leaves to the rounds. If you'd like, serve your breakfast with whole mint leaves on the side!

Food Fact!

Bruschetta is toasted or grilled Italian bread typically topped with olive oil, garlic, tomatoes, and basil. This recipe substitutes cream cheese for olive oil, honey for garlic, strawberries for tomatoes, and mint for basil!

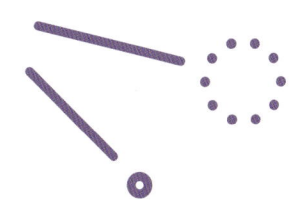

Mini Parfait Cups

These sweet mini parfaits make for a fun and easy breakfast. Top them with your favorite fruit!

Ingredients

vegetable oil
wonton wrappers
cinnamon
yogurt
strawberries, raspberries, peaches, pears, and other fruit

Supplies

basting brush
muffin tin
spoon
knife and cutting board

1. Preheat the oven to 375 degrees Fahrenheit (177°C).

2. Brush oil on both sides of each wrapper. Then sprinkle cinnamon on each side.

3. Carefully push a wrapper into each cup of the muffin tin.

4. Bake for eight minutes or until the wrappers are crispy and golden brown. Check that the bottom of each wrapper is crispy. Allow the wrappers to cool for five minutes before removing them from the tin.

5. Spoon yogurt into a wrapper, filling it one-third full. Repeat to fill the remaining wrappers.

6. Chop the fruit into bite-size pieces. Top the parfait cups with the fruit. Enjoy your sweet and crispy breakfast!

PB&J Oatmeal

Do you love peanut butter and jelly? Take this classic sandwich and turn it into a healthy, hearty breakfast.

Ingredients

½ cup rolled oats
½ cup milk
½ cup water
1 tablespoon peanut butter
1 tablespoon jelly
1 teaspoon peanuts (optional)
strawberries, halved (optional)

Supplies

measuring cups and spoons
microwave-safe bowl
spoon
knife and cutting board (optional)

1. Mix the rolled oats, milk, and water in the microwave-safe bowl.

2. Heat the oatmeal in the microwave for two minutes. Continue microwaving the oatmeal in 15-second increments until the oats are puffed and softened.

3. Stir the peanut butter and jelly into the oatmeal.

4. Top the oatmeal with peanuts and strawberries if you'd like!

Breakfast
Bagel Sandwiches

Take a simple bagel from ordinary to extraordinary with the help of eggs, cheese, and ham.

Ingredients

1 egg
salt and pepper to taste
1 teaspoon butter or
  vegetable oil
cheese slices
ham slices
large bagels or mini
  bagels

Supplies

bowl
whisk
measuring spoons
frying pan
spatula
plate
round cookie cutter

Food Tip

Make your bagel sandwich the night before! Wrap it in parchment paper and store it in the refrigerator overnight. In the morning, microwave the sandwich for 90 seconds.

1. Crack and whisk the egg in the bowl. Add salt and pepper.

2. Heat the butter or oil in the frying pan over medium heat.

3. Pour the egg into the frying pan.

4. When the edges of the egg start to brown (after about three minutes), flip the egg and let it cook for another minute. Then transfer the egg to the plate.

5. Warm the ham slices in the pan for one minute on each side.

6. Use the cookie cutter to cut circles out of the egg and the cheese.

7. Set an egg and cheese circle on one half of the bagel. Pile one or two ham slices on top. Top the sandwich with the other bagel half.

8. Repeat step 7 to make more bagel sandwiches. Enjoy!

Mug Omelet

This omelet could not be easier! Just crack an egg and add your favorite toppings to a mug for a simple and tasty breakfast.

Ingredients

¼ cup chopped toppings, such as ham, peppers, onion, and broccoli
1 egg
1 tablespoon milk
1 tablespoon grated cheese
salt and pepper to taste

Supplies

knife and cutting board
measuring cups and spoons
microwave-safe mug
fork

1. Put the toppings into the microwave-safe mug. Microwave the mug for two minutes.

2. Crack the egg into the mug.

3. Add the milk and cheese to the mug. Season with salt and pepper. Stir the mixture with the fork.

4. Microwave the mug for one minute. If the egg is runny, microwave the mug in 30-second increments until the egg is firm.

5. Your quick and easy omelet is ready to eat!

Breakfast Cookie Bars

Cookies for breakfast? It may sound too good to be true. But these hearty, healthy cookie bars make the perfect morning meal!

Ingredients

⅔ cup peanut butter
1½ tablespoons honey
¼ cup walnuts, chopped
1 tablespoon sunflower seeds
1 cup rolled oats
2 tablespoons shredded coconut
2 tablespoons semisweet chocolate chips
½ teaspoon vegetable oil

Supplies

measuring cups and spoons
mixing bowl
spoon
spatula
parchment paper
baking sheet
small microwave-safe bowl
knife

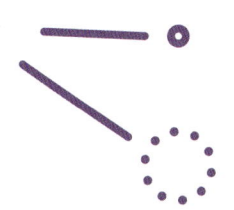

1. Mix the peanut butter and honey in the mixing bowl.

2. Add the walnuts, sunflower seeds, oats, and coconut to the mixing bowl. Stir until combined.

3. Spread the cookie mixture in a ½-inch (1.3-centimeter) layer on the parchment-lined baking sheet.

4. Mix the chocolate chips and oil in the microwave-safe bowl. Microwave the mixture in 15-second intervals, stirring between each one, until the chocolate is melted and smooth.

5. Drizzle the melted chocolate over the cookie mixture.

6. Put the baking sheet into the freezer for 10 minutes.

7. Remove the baking sheet from the freezer. Cut the cookie mixture into 2-by-3-inch (5-by-8-cm) bars.

8. If you'd like, wrap each cookie bar in parchment paper for a breakfast on the go. The parchment-wrapped bars can be stored in the refrigerator for up to one week!

Breakfast Tacos

Scrambled eggs are a breakfast staple. Use them as the base for delicious breakfast tacos!

Ingredients

2 eggs
2 precooked breakfast
  sausage links
1 teaspoon olive or
  vegetable oil
4 crunchy taco shells
¼ cup shredded cheese
½ cup shredded lettuce
¼ cup salsa

Supplies

mixing bowl
whisk
knife and cutting board
frying pan
measuring cups and
  spoons
spatula
spoon

1. Crack the eggs into the mixing bowl and whisk them.

2. Cut the sausages into bite-size pieces and add them to the eggs.

3. Heat the oil in the frying pan over medium heat.

4. Pour the egg and sausage mixture into the pan. Stir periodically with the spatula until the eggs are firm.

5. Scoop the scrambled eggs into the taco shells. Top your breakfast tacos with cheese, lettuce, and salsa!

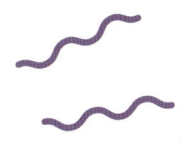

Breakfast Quesadilla

Put a fun spin on a classic appetizer with this loaded breakfast quesadilla.

Ingredients

1 tablespoon olive or
  vegetable oil
2 eggs
2 tablespoons bell pepper,
  chopped
1 tablespoon onion,
  chopped
2 large flour tortillas
1 teaspoon butter
2 tablespoons precooked
  bacon, crumbled
¼ cup shredded cheese
shredded lettuce
  (optional)
avocado slices (optional)
salsa (optional)

Supplies

knife and cutting board
measuring cups and
  spoons
frying pan
spatula
plate
microwave-safe bowl
serving plate

1. Heat the oil in the frying pan over medium heat. Crack the eggs into the pan and stir them.

2. Flip the eggs when the edges are brown and crispy. Let them cook for one more minute. Then slide the cooked eggs onto the plate.

3. Microwave the pepper and onion for two minutes in the microwave-safe bowl.

4. While the pepper and onion cook, butter one side of each tortilla. Place one tortilla butter side down in the pan.

5. Sprinkle half the cheese on top of the tortilla. Set the egg on the cheese. Then sprinkle the pepper, onion, bacon, and  remaining cheese on top. Place the other tortilla on top, butter side up.

6. Check the bottom tortilla after four minutes. When it begins to brown, flip the quesadilla.

7. Cook the other side for two minutes or until golden brown. Then transfer the quesadilla to the serving plate.

8. Cut the quesadilla into wedges. Serve it with shredded lettuce, avocado slices, and salsa if you'd like!

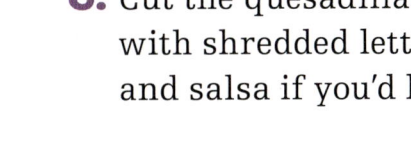

French Toast
Waffles

Combine two mouthwatering breakfasts
into one with this simple recipe.

Ingredients

2 eggs
2 tablespoons milk
1 teaspoon cinnamon
1 teaspoon brown sugar
vegetable oil spray
4 slices bread
maple syrup (optional)
fresh fruit (optional)

Supplies

mixing bowl
measuring spoons
whisk
waffle iron
fork
plate

1. Crack the eggs into the mixing bowl. Whisk in the milk, cinnamon, and brown sugar.

2. Heat the waffle iron. Spray it with oil spray.

3. Quickly dip one slice of bread into the egg mixture. Lift the bread up to let excess egg mixture drip off.

4. Place the bread in the waffle iron. Close the top.

5. Let the bread cook until steam stops rising from the waffle iron (after about three minutes). Use the fork to remove the waffle from the waffle iron. Place the waffle on the plate.

6. Repeat steps 3 through 5 with the remaining slices of bread.

7. If you'd like, serve your French toast waffles with maple syrup and fresh fruit!

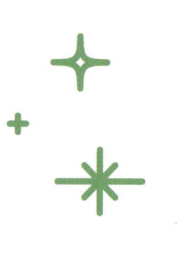

Almond Flour Pancakes

Protein packed and delicious to eat, almond flour pancakes are a great twist on a traditional favorite.

Food Tip

Almond pancakes are more fragile than regular pancakes, so small pancakes are easier to flip!

Ingredients

1⅓ cup almond flour, plus more if needed

1 teaspoon baking powder

¼ teaspoon salt

¼ cup almond milk, plus more if needed

2 large eggs

1 tablespoon pure maple syrup

1 teaspoon vanilla

1 tablespoon oil or butter, plus extra

maple syrup for serving (optional)

blueberries (optional)

Supplies

measuring cups and spoons

2 mixing bowls

spoon

frying pan

spatula

1. In a large mixing bowl, stir together the almond flour, baking powder, and salt.

2. In a small mixing bowl, stir together the almond milk, eggs, maple syrup, and vanilla.

3. Pour the wet ingredients into the bowl with the dry ingredients and stir. If you'd like thinner pancakes, stir in 1 tablespoon almond milk at a time until the batter thins. If you'd like thicker pancakes, stir in 1 tablespoon almond flour at a time until the batter thickens.

4. Heat the oil or butter in the frying pan over medium heat. Pour ¼ cup batter into the pan for each pancake.

5. When the pancakes are done bubbling, use the spatula to carefully flip them. Let the pancakes cook for another minute.

6. Repeat steps 4 and 5 using the remaining pancake batter. Add more oil or butter to the pan if necessary.

7. If you'd like, serve your almond pancakes with maple syrup and blueberries!

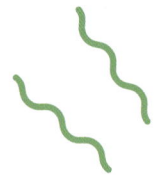
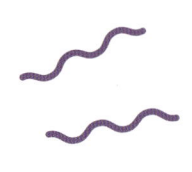

Baked Donuts

Have a little more than 15 minutes? Bake up a batch of delicious donuts for a sweet breakfast!

Ingredients

1 cup all-purpose or almond flour
½ tablespoon baking powder
2 tablespoons brown sugar
¼ teaspoon salt
½ teaspoon cinnamon
1 egg
¼ cup vegetable oil
1 cup milk
½ teaspoon vanilla
vegetable oil spray
frosting (optional)
sprinkles (optional)

Supplies

measuring cups and spoons
2 mixing bowls
whisk
donut pan

Food Tip

Make a donut pan with a muffin tin and aluminum foil! Take a square piece of foil and fold the center around your finger. Remove your finger and place the foil in a muffin cup. Repeat to fill all the cups!

1. Preheat the oven to 350 degrees Fahrenheit (177°C).

2. Whisk together the flour, baking powder, brown sugar, salt, and cinnamon in a large mixing bowl.

3. Whisk together the egg, oil, milk, and vanilla in a medium mixing bowl.

4. Add the wet mixture to the dry ingredients and mix well.

5. Spray the donut pan with oil spray.

6. Pour the batter into the donut pan, filling each cavity about three-fourths full.

7. Bake the donuts for 12 minutes or until golden brown.

8. Decorate the donuts with your favorite toppings, such as frosting and sprinkles!

Read More

Borgert-Spaniol, Megan. *Tasty Meals in 15 Minutes or Less*. North Mankato, MN: Capstone, 2024.

Green, Gail. *Breakfast Recipe Queen*. North Mankato, MN: Capstone, 2019.

Oringer, Verveine. *Cooking with My Dad, the Chef: 70+ Kid-Tested, Kid-Approved (and Gluten-Free!) Recipes for Young Chefs!* Boston: America's Test Kitchen, 2023.

Internet Sites

Breakfast
kidshealth.org/en/kids/breakfast.html

Is Breakfast Really the Most Important Meal of the Day?
wonderopolis.org/wonder/Is-Breakfast-Really-the-Most-Important-Meal-of-the-Day

Kids' Breakfast Recipes
bbcgoodfood.com/recipes/collection/kids-breakfast-recipes

About the Author

Tami grew up eating only peanut butter and jelly sandwiches and mac and cheese. It wasn't until she was an adult that food sparked her interest. Since then, she has thrown herself into trying new foods and improving every recipe she can find. She lives in Minnesota with her husband, two daughters, and a big orange cat.